Trou

TROUBLE

By Alison Winch

WITH AN INTRODUCTION
BY SARAH HOWE

THE EMMA PRESS

First published in Great Britain in 2016 by the Emma Press Ltd

Reprinted in 2018

Poems copyright © Alison Winch 2016
Introduction copyright © Sarah Howe 2016
Cover illustration copyright © Sophie Herxheimer 2016

ISBN 978-1-910139-39-4

A CIP catalogue record of this book
is available from the British Library.

Printed and bound in Great Britain
by Impact Print, Hereford.

The Emma Press
theemmapress.com
hello@theemmapress.com
Birmingham, UK

Introduction

'Here comes trouble', the saying goes: harder to pin down than worry or strife, 'trouble' marks a downturn in one's fortunes, of course, but often has an extra edge of something like naughtiness, cheek – the thrill of a ruin you pursue in full knowledge. Its 'Here comes...' variety has an undertow of sexiness: the *femme fatale* sauntering by in the movies, the hot, charismatic guy in the office you really shouldn't... Trouble, in all these senses, is just around the corner in this first pamphlet from Alison Winch. Her poems are, by turns, lyrical, erotic, funny, tender, blunt, baroquely wrought and extremely moving:

Trouble

this flesh against the tobacco fruit of your lip,
still sweet with the syrup blister of Yamazaki [...]

This comes from the poem that lends its name to the pamphlet, whose run-on title spills into the opening lines, unable to contain its ominous luxuriance. Reminiscent of a stylist like Brenda Shaughnessy, the sheer sensuous splendour of Winch's language has an air of fallenness, as if the 'fruit of your lip' had touched, moments before, an Edenic apple. Her syntax wrong-foots us across the gap, as what seems at first a noun morphs into an un-disobeyable imperative, a caress: 'Trouble / this flesh...'

This pivoting moment is typical of Winch's fascination with the mechanics of attention, within poems that advertise their tongue-in-cheek openness to distraction: 'On this body is a head, I explain, and in this head is a pack of spaniels, a pack so dense they are a mind. And they fawn over men.' *Trouble* develops a phenomenology of passion, minutely cataloguing the varieties of 'want', from sexual desire ('I want him down in this impish wood') to the speaker's fierce, protective care for an elderly grandmother ('I want to hold her here / ...under this balcony, and never let her go'). The sensibility conjured by these poems is, at once, extravagantly romantic and disaffectedly mordant:

'O Kingsland Road. O bus.' The poems in *Trouble* are open to the seductions of flesh, but also to the seductions of language, the mouth-feel of its sounds: 'Remember... the way you / circled your tongue around the salt prod of his cock.'

Many of Winch's poems chart the fissures and shifts in communication between two, intimate humans. The seesaw of male-female power relations plays out against the theatrical backdrop of an analyst's couch, complete with all the props of erotic fantasy, in the prose-poem sequence 'Of Wife'. As a character type, its marriage counsellor has some of Emily Berry's biographer in his DNA, reappearing sometimes in a foppish, eighteenth-century fancy dress: 'He chews on pigeon pie and admires his coat buttons. Then he inserts his fingers into my ribcage and scoops out the nightingale that sings just above my spleen.' Winch's range is evident from the way poems in a bang-contemporary idiom sit alongside the studied archaism of 'Alisoun's', a sequence giving new voice to a character 'appropriated' from Chaucer's *Miller's Tale*. Its raunchy, Middle English-inflected rhythms drive this experiment in persona – Alisoun as the mask of Alison – whose brio and vivid diction achieve something far beyond pastiche: 'lyfe's caul fuse / this newte that ruts in the pond of my uterus / plip plop plunge'.

Alongside 'Expecting, the Gourd', still another sequence extracted in *Trouble*, these are some of the best recent poems of impending motherhood I've seen. Winch evokes the child swelling, gourd-like, in the womb with a rollicking unsentimentality that stages its own quiet, political intervention. That poem's recurring botanical metaphors, budding with new life, supply a moving counterpoint to the series of plant-named poems ('Magnolia', 'Hops', 'Pomegranate', 'Potato') which chart the demise of an elderly relative: 'Incontinence pads dot our flat / like fallen bracts.'

Winch's poems chart a swerving, yet ever-sure course through troubled waters. Hers is a fearless and impenitent new voice. Reader, I'm glad you've found your way to this extraordinary debut.

Sarah Howe
MAY 2016

Contents

from *Of Wife*

I. On the Manner in which Wife introduces Her Self

The marriage counsellor has me sit on his chaise longue, behind him a long green garden like a secret glade. I pretend to be one woman.

On this body is a head, I explain, and in this head is a pack of spaniels, a pack so dense they are a mind. And they fawn over men. Men made up of golden light, muddy crystals, kissing cherries.

Trouble

for B.

this flesh against the tobacco fruit of your lip,
still sweet with the syrup blister of Yamazaki;
demand and relent the bed's length
with a perseverance that steers us.

The porcelain glaze of your eyes is wet
with love as we square up to dark and win.
At eight, we run at a clean city
rinsing itself in April. O Kingsland Road. O bus.

Eastbourne

We're the youngest guests at the Queen's Hotel –
and you're 52. It's the summer solstice and we're breaking up

except we're making love on the fifth floor
in an evening light as yolky as an afternoon.

The sexy doom of the split
is like falling in love and a stay of execution.

Everything's alive: whelks, do-nuts.
The soupy fumblings of the sea.

Just a day trip to Seven Sisters,
without the bookies – you clot with nostalgia

for our first months, sharbing in Tottenham:
Ladbrokes, William Hill, Paddy Power.

The wind touches us up as we tussle
in the purple gorse,

the beam of the bitten cliffs,
and Eastbourne: ballroom dancing, plastic bed sheets, eggnog.

Women whose hearts are clamped on their faces
hard as wedding bands.   Driving home

(it's no longer ours) we stop at Pease Pottage services:
a piece of the universe that love forgot.

ii. The Tea Table

When the marriage counsellor kissed me we were in the long eighteenth century (our borough didn't exist then, not our flat, not our street).

He availed himself of a flagon of pear wine and enlightened me on the characteristics of men, their manners, tastes, opinions. The bell tolled noon. As he stood his pink curved heels gave him a rakish height. I leaned in to taste his painted lips, stained as they were with snuff and pear and tannin. *Innocent like a nymph*, he murmured, or *shepherdess*.

O.

My cheeks flushed with immodest blood as I patted his cheek with a fan. My dress was green. The flowers on the bow porcelain teapot trembled as he artfully gloved my left breast. The sugar bowl spilt on the pastoral cloth and the panniers on my skirt shoved the tea caddy as he groped the charms of my garter.

I was wet the whole time!

(There are private spaces in public places and this knowledge is dangerous if you are a below-par Wife.)

My Generous Host

after Charles Baudelaire

He bids me follow him into a subterranean dwelling of astonishing
luxury: Ladbrokes. I smell of climes; my eyes are sunset and aurora.
We spend an eternal afternoon as if on an island of melodious
cascades. If I had a spouse and household, I would forget them.

We perch as lovers; copious libations cut through with roll-ups on
Green Lanes. I gain and waste my soul with heroic carelessness: dogs,
horses, European tournaments. It is like losing someone else's worry.

IV. THE BALLROOM

The theme for today is the unspoken contract in every marriage.

– *So, my ruddy wench?* he strokes the head of his sword and takes advantage of the French claret.
– *You stay in the eighteenth century releasing my breasts from whalebone and I put up a fervent resistance.*
He chews on pigeon pie and admires his coat buttons. Then he inserts his fingers into my ribcage and scoops out the nightingale that sings just above my spleen. Shoving the bird into my cupped hands, he stalks to the back of the ballroom.

– *Ye Gods, make it sing for me!* he roars from underneath a candelabra, *with a full throat, as if on a ******* bough.*

The nightingale fibrillates its sweetness as I shift my contouche, *Louder*, I whisper, *make it a high requiem!*

When I look up the marriage counsellor is waltzing with a countess. He blows a kiss over her shoulder. *Dine on roasted larks*; he gestures at a long table arrayed with a fine seduction of sweet meats and thick beer.

Draupadi Goes on a Greek Holiday

after Paul Muldoon's 'The Little Black Book'

In our rented Yaris, Pete cops a feel between my legs.
Elvis Pelvis hips, and a steering wheel between my legs.

Nick's soft on ouzo and souvlaki.
Al fresco, he knocks up a meal between my legs.

Athlete Chris has scabs on his knees and jealous groupies.
He bleeds as he tries to kneel between my legs.

Jack's flat is squeezed with planks and vodka.
His paintbrush strokes surreal between my legs.

We spit cherry stones at the Aegean sea.
The shore's salty lip, and Neil between my legs.

Tonight I conjure the unreal between my legs.
All Draupadi's husbands will reveal between my legs.

Alisoun's

Via Francigena, Italy 13—

Arse – myne! – that's how you know me
that & my wenching – but dear Lord what an arse!
like the dymple blush of a just-plucked pear
plump on its honybee haunches
when the kitchen is a lyht box of morning sonne

*

Your harlotry! Cuckoldom! scolded the Carpenter
the scholar & Absolon –

*

A colty weasel flash along the beck / my staff & scrip
spiced ale & cake
a blisse slip pilgrim slopping to Rome –

'A woman will receive *[...]*
males:/ No prick agains*[t]*
her lust prevails./ For
who could fill his spous*[e]*
spout?/ Alone she wear*[s]*
the district out.' (Again
Marrying c. 1222-50)

Love-longynge: earth has chylded itself
spryng-rynsed in its own deawes mucus

a river busts aumbyr
wet fenyl smell of shut cupped dayes-eyes / sprung moss

I chew at the air's colossal fizz
its gentil gorse

the sonne's pancake mouth at my face
& the path dots with forget-me-knots

O love-lorn mourns at my loyns – *Nicholas!*

I want him down in this impish wood
its wayside shrynes / its dance of hazylnuts –

I zest with two hertes
more of me to canker or revel

lyfe's caul fuse
this newte that ruts in the pond of my uterus
plip plop plunge – *Rakehell*!

my cunt whystle-flutes
like crushable fowls
woo poppys & primeroles after morning rain –

my proselytism's
to wet nettles
& Poseiden who drags like the moone swyves the sea

Spanking! he bondaged to feel the passiun of muscle
my myt without murder – *Dirty Dog*!

he pelts my mind – Nicholas – as May's cuckoo spyt
pysse-drys to June

below the river's a pour of mellow wine
that cools the caterwaul cockles of my bihynde

*'Every woman is
further polluted by the
vice of disobedience.'
(Andreas Capellanus,
c. 1180)*

O perfect seede shooting from prodygyous cooks!
the dotard Carpenter rankles still

his glooms / old meat
his recitations *Of Wykked Wyves*

you can bette
cake

never fairly divides
between husband & wyf –

I'm not lyquorysh sold in a market
or a basyn or washbole or stool or spoon – No!

your payne is not woman (cherysh me)
or mydenhood

but the wrecched love of property – *confound you*!
(like this newte is not myne but its own self's the leaves' the sky's)

Uxorial I coupled a coquillard under a bedde faked by roots of a pyne tree
our counterfeit gorged my gadget
as if I could tryk him into something real

February fat crowes steered through slackened flakes
my empty stoupe wrecced against clouds
that plodded a blue sky like the vertebrae of an ox

sonne bloode over Besançon – black hair salted a cross
from nipple to navel & me on my knees
soft palate open like a Roman duomo his hand at my neck & the snowe –

*coquillard – pseudo pilgrim, so named because they wore a scallop shell to disguise
their fraudulent intentions*

12

Not Nicholas Absolon
nor the Carpenter

it was the coquillard
with his scallope shelle

who robbed me of almes
& accommodations

& left me a womb bud
a pox payn

like a baker's dozen
of Absolon's pokers

the bob-bobness of Nicholas'
knendyng-tubbes –

*Now just as mankind is the
most perfect of all animals, so
within mankind the man is
more perfect than the woman.'
(Galen, 131-201)*

*

Lo
perfectyon isn't real

like *gammon* or *buttercup*
or *purple iris*

but a rule
like *god* or *wyf*

Dimwits!
Eue was born of the noblest

(Adames bon & blod)
& in a terrestrial paradise –

see her vesselle's soule
fooles see her soule…

'the mother provides the
matter of the body which
receives its form only by
means of the power which
is contained in the father's
seed' (St Thomas Aquinas,
1225-1274)

Shush those who speak badde of woman!
I'm no scholar like Nicholas

nor godely
(but there's only one of me)
this is it

only the imperfect yeast
of love

spiderwebs   hermytes   wyte truffles
leprosarium & geltatello that pley this path

& bygging with my belly's swampe
not god's miracle

but that marshland newte this quym my arse –

geltatello – orphans

15

Disciple

In spring the clouds were the sunlit backs of lazy otters.
White irises bent
against the rain and the trees' rotting lemons.

The guru was my truth across the cold afternoons.
To him I was as clear as a glass of raki,
its lippy prints and finger stains.

My spite was a wasp slipping the rim.
He repositioned my thoughts till they were other people's
and in the olive grove, nets dipped like funeral veils.

I sat at the feet of the guru all summer,
as my ego flashed in and out of the world like a firefly:
figs were the bruised balls of Greek statues coming

alive all over the British Museum;
green leaves were three fat thumbs.
I sent a postcard of peninsulars to thank a woman for birthing me.

When he left on his path as *bodhisattva*
with my phone number and a punnet of peaches
I bawled, *But I need you.*

Then I removed the flint from my core
and drew it across his throat –
every thing has an aura: cows   the sea   artichokes.

Magnolia

The cold has broken open
and the saucer magnolia at the end of the hall
is in an ancient bloom.

We are standing
to the bathroom, and my grandmother drowns
in the crook of my arm

as we relax in the texture of carpet and feet.
The tree is leafless
in a distant land, its sepals are silk light bulbs.

Incontinence pads dot our flat
like fallen bracts.
Red flowers spill from their pegs on the pocket handkerchief tree

as clouds relieve themselves over the pagoda
and the sun falls
through branches of a tropical Redwood: yellow linoleum.

Hops

We see them from the fifth tier of our pagoda.
Strung up on the yard's struts,
their long green arms pinned like mannequins';
a field of thin-limbed brides.
       I was like them, she murmurs. *Tall.*

Since her release from Keats Ward and her fall
in the spring, we've been talking at fractures,
a dowager's hump
as she dodders mute on milk pudding feet.

       But he picked me. Remember?
And she sinks back into the sofa, staring at the hops
as they flutter on surrogate spines.

Russell Square

We lie in a green incubator,
disinfecting our souls with chlorophyll.

We've been scavenging at the back
side of yellow lines

in this city's tubes for too many lives.
The sun is ignoring us

but the sky is ours; yellow roses, ash trees,
sycamores are ours

and nectarine stones, pear cores.
We've been in repose

since the scraggy dawn
handed herself in;

it's Tuesday
and we've surrendered our 9am.

This is all we have.
Our souls are not birds,

they are sluttishly coupled
to these bodies, their chins, verrucas.

Pomegranate

I press it with both thumbs,
cracking its arils
so its insides fracture into a sack of sap.

She rests her palm on my back as I squash
the ball into juice and prick
its leathery skin, squirting ruby fluid for swallowing opiates.

The honeycomb mesh of her spine
is breaking up, but her skin still blooms
at my touch, its electric flecks.

rom *Expecting, the Gourd*

'Pregnancy – the temporary deformation of the body of the individual for the sake of the species – is barbaric.' – Shulamith Firestone

wallows and golden orioles soar through bedrooms
riezed in copulating lovers: the fertility villa.
Note polycystic ovaries and oleander bushes. Remember
he ovulation cycle, wonky uterus, the way you
ircled your tongue around the salt prod of his cock.
This is your bed now lie in it: ectopic pregnancies,
Bacchus, Pan, folic acid. All your hang-ups will pass to your child.
He'll spur you here with all the kisses of his mouth. It is your choice –

***

after Arthur Rimbaud

Like kissing the peachy cheek of a chambermaid,
delicate ankles, strawberry-raspberry taste, her flowery flesh – *I love you!*
And then the pox: *Ugly whore!*
You're puking cabbage-green skies like a drunk
without romance:
ulcerous anus, swollen tits, a snatch no one wants – this is morning sickness!
Only oat cakes and ire
to whip one through to the end of each perverted day.

***

Cross-legged I try to winch it out of myself,
his breath a greased machine of *metta*
hoisting it from the waste of wench flesh,

he tedium of a winch mind: tripe and peas,

fighting bracelets, a saint's feet warmed by otters.
I want to swing: pure, clean, free of Gourd.

****

Gourd makes me eat again, mimics Hofuku:
Have you had your dinner?
We seek the cool of buses en route to Homerton hospital,
the seats' pelt is lotus flowers –
I'm a secret eater, I am what I eat, I'm alone like a rhinoceros horn.

Afterwards, Gourd hauls me down to the Meccano blue chairs
of Chicken Dome on Holloway Road
as it's kinder to be carnivorous when it's mainly squash –
its hair is salty rind; we oil the formica, fingers,
belly's orb – who knows what a body can do.

Potato

Found broken in a thick spread of ashes,
you're suspended
twenty three thousand years in the future.

Bits of you are missing
but each time I visit
you've enlarged your body's parameters into obesity

and are glorious:
heavy breasts of mammoth ivory,
fatty folds of a lower abdomen and back, vulva slit.

You are sculpted out of your self
so your eyes are oval depressions
and your scent a skillet of potatoes, frying.

All the Affairs are with my Grandmother

I rise and seek about the city,
on the underground and down Euston Road
among the commuters who giddy
their wings in this Tuesday morning bowl of springlight.
It is March. I want to hold her here
on Ossulston Street

under this balcony, and never let her go.
I'd let her kiss me, old and dead as she is.
This is our bed. Under the cold sun of a budded ash,
her hands on my sleeve, her head on my cheek.
We are the fibrillations of a palm-size bird;
cloud salad, sky cranes, green canopy.

NOTES

Alisoun is a character appropriated from Geoffrey Chaucer's *The Miller's Tale*. The Via Francigena is a medieval pilgrim route from Canterbury to Rome.

Draupadi is a figure from the Mahabharata. She had five husbands, all brothers.

ACKNOWLEDGEMENTS

Thanks are due to the editors of the following print and online publications in which some of these poems first appeared: *ink sweat and tears, Long Poem Magazine, Magma, Poetry Wales, Rabbit, The New Writer*.

Love and thanks to my friends, poet-sharers and teachers. I am especially indebted to those who commented on the manuscript – Stuart Cooke, Peter Daniels, Sophie Herxheimer, Clare Pollard, Kate Potts and Natania Rosenfeld. Special thanks also to Emma Wright and Rachel Piercey at the Emma Press, to Sarah Howe for writing the introduction, and to Sophie for the cover image. I am grateful for a Hawthornden Fellowship in June 2014. This pamphlet is dedicated, with love, to Ben.

ABOUT THE POET

Alison Winch is a lecturer in Media Studies at the University of East Anglia. She is author of *Girlfriends and Postfeminist Sisterhood* (Palgrave, 2013) and co-editor of *Encountering Buddhism in Twentieth-Century British and American Literature* (Bloomsbury, 2013).

THE EMMA PRESS

small press, big dreams

The Emma Press is an independent publisher dedicated to producing beautiful, thought-provoking books. It was founded in 2012 by Emma Wright in Winnersh, UK, and is now based in Birmingham. Having been shortlisted in both 2014 and 2015, the Emma Press won the Michael Marks Award for Poetry Pamphlet Publishers in 2016.

The Emma Press is passionate about making poetry welcoming and accessible. In 2015 they received a grant from Arts Council England to travel around the country with Myths and Monsters, a tour of poetry readings and workshops for children. They are often on the lookout for new writing and run regular calls for submissions to their themed poetry anthologies and poetry pamphlet series.

Sign up to the monthly Emma Press newsletter to hear about their events, publications and upcoming calls for submissions. Their books are available to buy from the online shop, as well as in bookshops.

theemmapress.com
emmavalleypress.blogspot.co.uk

OTHER EMMA PRESS POETRY PAMPHLETS

PAISLEY, *by Rakhshan Rizwan* / ISBN: 978 1 910139 78 3

Rakhshan Rizwan's debut collection simmers with a poised, driving anger.

PISANKI, *by Zosia Kuczyńska* / ISBN: 978 1 910139 72 1

Kuczyńska's poems are both richly narrative and sharply attentive to the complexities of home and culture.

WHO SEEMED ALIVE & ALTOGETHER REAL
    by Padraig Regan / ISBN: 978 1 910139 74 5

This pamphlet is alive with the textures of paint, sweat, sugar and overripe fruit.

MACKEREL SALAD, *by Ben Rogers*
ISBN: 978 1 910139 41 7

The poems of *Mackerel Salad* explore maps, being lost, trying to hide, and the nature of exploration itself.

GOOSE FAIR NIGHT, *by Kathy Pimlott*
ISBN: 978 1 910139 35 6

A generous, jellied feast of a book, full of sharp yet tender details about friendship, family and familiarity.

RASPBERRIES FOR THE FERRY, *by Andrew Wynn Owen*
ISBN: 978 0 9574596 5 6

Andrew Wynn Owen dazzles in his debut pamphlet, whisking the reader up with his infectious rhythms and lively sensuality.